Bygone GALASHIELS

by

Norman Henderson

This shop was at "Combats Corner" in Market Street. Most of the building, which included the original Kings Temperance Hotel, was demolished to help widen the road at the junction of Market Street and Bank Street.

ISBN 1-872074-24-3

First Published in the United Kingdom, 1993
By Richard Stenlake, Ochiltree Sawmill, The Lade, Ochiltree, Ayrshire KA18 2NX
Telephone: 02907 266

INTRODUCTION

Galashiels has many claims to distinction. Capital of the "Scott Country" and the chief administrative centre of Selkirkshire, it was one of the principal seats of the woollen industry in Scotland, justly famed throughout the world for the quality and variety of its tweeds. The Braw Lads Gathering, held at Galashiels in mid-summer every year, is one of the most colourful festivals of its kind in Scotland and the local war memorial, with its clocked tower and magnificent equestrian statue, has few rivals.

The name of the town comes from the old British word *gwala*, meaning full or fast stream, and *shiels,* a Saxon word for shelter or hut. The form of the name has changed many times over the centuries and these are but a few of the many variations:

Galche (1124)   Galashel (1337)   Gala (1559)

      Gallawshells (1633)   Galasheils or Galashiels (1714)

The earliest historical mention of Galashiels occurs in 1337, when, legend has it, that a party of English soldiers, gathering wild plums near the confluence of the Rivers Tweed and Gala, were surprised by local men who "cut them off to a man". Their bodies were thrown into a trench situated in Eastlands, known as the Englishman's Syke and marked by a large boulder called The Raid Stane. In commemoration of this exploit, the inhabitants of the village who had taken part in the attack adopted the title of "Soor Plooms of Galashiels", now included in the coat-of-arms of the burgh.

The lands and Manor of Galashiels formed part of Ettrick Forest and were granted to Sir James Pringle by Robert Bruce in 1321. When the kings of Scotland hunted in the forest they occupied a lodge at Galashiels which was known as "Hunters Ha".

Galashiels was originally in the Parish of Lindean and for some centuries the church stood there, nearly half-way to Selkirk. It has been suggested that it was founded from Old Melrose, but it was served from about 1126 by the monks of Kelso and was one of many Borders churches in their charge. Towards the end of the 16th century the Vicar of Lindean resided in Galashiels, by then a small village, and in 1586 the church was abandoned. John Knox's widow, Margaret Stewart, is one of those buried within its walls. The second site of the church was at Baleside, a good deal nearer to Galashiels. Later, the Tolbooth, erected about 1599 after Galashiels became a burgh, served as a place of public worship, until 1617 when a third church was built on the Selkirk road to the south of Gala House. All that is left of this church is the small part known as the Scott (Gala) Aisle, which, apart from Old Gala House, is the oldest surviving building in Galashiels. It was erected by Captain Hugh Scott, a younger son of the renowned Borderer "Wat of Harden", his mother being Mary Scott "The Rose of Yarrow", who was then laird of Gala. He died on 1st September 1644 and his tomb lies within the Aisle. The Parish of Lindean was formally changed to the Parish of Galashiels in 1562 as a result of the latter having become the main village in the area.

The village of Galashiels subsequently developed slowly although by 1790 there was a thriving cottage industry with 43 looms at work and about 240 women spinning yarn. But it was the revolution in textile production of the late 18th and early 19th centuries which really brought Galashiels to prominence. The introduction of new machinery for woollen cloth manufacture gave an impetus to trade. Machines were bought that did the work of hand-carders and the spinning wheel was suddenly obsolete. Small mills began to spring up and new ideas worked out. Mills were constantly enlarged to cope with the ever growing demand. Communication with the cities quickened as the railway at last ran through the town in 1849. The tweed trade was fast becoming an important and valuable part of the United Kingdom's commerce and prosperity. This trade, which grew to be the main business of most of the Borders towns, was generally accepted as having its origin in Galashiels.

Much of the credit for the emergence of Galashiels as a main tweed manufacturing town must go to Dr. Robert Douglas, the Parish Minister for the 50 years from 1770-1820. When he first came, the town was a quiet country village. In 1780 the population was just 900. When he died, in 1820, it was a thriving and rapidly growing town with an international reputation and a rapidly growing population (by 1865 it had risen to 7500 and the 1891 census recorded over 17,000 inhabitants). He has frequently been described as "The Founder of Modern Galashiels". He freely lent his own money insisting that the manufacturers should have the newest and best machinery. After the Napoleonic Wars there was a general depression of all industry, especially textiles, and factory closures were numerous. It was at this time of need that Dr. Douglas again came forward and by his personal credit enabled the manufacturers of Galashiels to weather the recession.

The textile industry is no longer such a dominant factor in the local economy, but its influence can still be seen around the town. The world famous Scottish College of Textiles is still the required learning centre for students from all over Britain and abroad. Peter Anderson's produces the world's largest range of pure wool worsted tartans at Nether Mill, which was built in 1805 and is a listed building. This mill now incorporates the Galashiels Museum and a 40 minute guided tour can be arranged. In the Market Square, once the commercial centre of Galashiels during the town's growth in the early years of the last century, stands a modern statue of a shepherd carrying a sheep on his shoulders – a symbol perhaps of days now past when Galashiels was so dependent on wool for its development and prosperity.

A group of Galashiels weavers posing with their shuttles and weft pirns.

JUBILEE OF THE OPENING OF THE SELKIRK BRANCH 5|4|06

Plans for a railway from Edinburgh to Galashiels were made in the early part of the 1800s, but it was not until 1844, after a public meeting in the Bridge Inn, that it was agreed to support the enterprise. A labour force of up to 1000 navvies was employed and by August 1848 the line had reached as far as Bowland. Coaches were run from Galashiels to Bowland on Lammas Fair Day that year so that the people of Galashiels could take a day trip to Edinburgh. 1849 saw the line open through Galashiels and St. Boswells to Hawick. "The Border Union Railway", as it was called then, was renamed "The Waverley Route" after the line was extended to Carlisle by the North British Railway. An extensive branch-line network quickly followed. The line to Selkirk opened in April 1856 and another line north of the town reached Peebles in June 1866.

Goods train crash in Galashiels yard, 1908. The Portobello and Kelso goods, leaving Galashiels to travel on up the line to Carlisle, failed to stop at Dawn Home Signal with this tragic result.

The retaining walls just below Ladhope tunnel had been a source of concern to railway engineers for some time and repairs to cracks in the walls were begun in the autumn of 1916. But on the 14th December workmen noticed more cracks appearing and had barely time to leave the site when a seventy yard stretch of the wall gave way, bringing down thousands of tons of rock and soil which completely blocked the railway line. Trains had to terminate at Bowland for the next few days, travellers going to and from Galashiels by bus until the tunnel was re-opened.

An A 3 Pacific No. 2745 4-6-2 'Captain Cuttle' entering Galashiels Station in the early 1930s. On the left is the Abbotsford Hotel with Brownlee's Garage behind. Barely visible "above" the roof of the garage is the "Coffee-Pot" Gala-Selkirk train, waiting for the main line to get clear before commencing its run down into the station.

Even as early as this, the growth of road transport was having a serious effect on railway finances and branch line closures had begun. The "Lauder Light Railway", opened as recently as 1901, lots its passenger service through Oxton to Fountainhall in September 1932. Duns and Selkirk branches were closed to passengers in September 1951 although freight continued until 1964. The Peebles route closed completely in February 1962. With all the branch lines closed the Waverley Line was left for a short time on its own until it too fell under the Beeching axe in 1969.

Left: At a meeting on 29th September 1833 a local businessman, Mr. Robert Gill, moved "that the town be lighted with gas and that a Company should be formed for the purpose". This was unanimously accepted and the necessary steps were taken at once to carry out the scheme. A gasworks was set up in Paton Street and by 1848 100 gas lamps had been erected in the town. In 1866 the Gas Company moved from Paton Street to their present location at Galafoot. The showroom shown here, in the High Street, served the town for many years until moving to new premises in Channel Street.

Right: Forte's Cafe in Market Street circa 1930.

This billiards room formed part of Forte's Cafe in Market Street. It boasted several full size tables and was a popular meeting place for the town's menfolk until its closure.

MRS. PROVOST RUTHERFORD CUTTING FIRST SOD, GALASHIELS SEWERAGE WORKS

After many years of delay and much controversy about the desirability of building a sewage works in Galashiels, work did eventually begin on the project in 1908. It was completed in 1912 and properties in the town were connected to the new system over the subsequent few years. Previously, sewage disposal had always been a problem, with the bulk of the sewage (known as 'street manure') being collected in carts and then moved by rail to a local farm.

Galashiels   *Channel Street*

Channel Street circa 1904. Fifty years previously none of what we see here even existed. At the far left of the street Mr. William Patterson built a tannery, situated between Channel Street and Overhaugh Street. A row of houses opposite, of which Mr. Patterson himself owned forty-nine, was known as Tannage Street and housed the workers of the tannery. A great deal of water was required for the factory and this was diverted from the mill lade to run through the building. When it emerged at the other side it ran open down the street before entering the Gala. It became known as the Tannery Burn or The Channel so that when the street was developed it was naturally named Channel Street. Patterson never married and the tannery closed down after his death.

The burning of Victoria Mills
Clapperton, Photo Galashiels

Victoria Mills were completely destroyed by this June 1905 fire. The mill was not rebuilt and the site was used for the building of the South of Scotland Technical College which was duly opened in September 1909. Of a total cost of £21,000, the Burgh School Board raised £11,000 through a public appeal and the balance was supplied by the Scottish Education Department.

BANK STREET, GALASHIELS, IN FLOOD,
27TH JUNE, 1905.

Incredibly, the day after the Victoria Mills fire, Galashiels was hit by a severe storm. Roads were washed away and landslides occurred throughout the district.

Mr. George Craig, who was Scott of Gala's "Baron Bailie" from 1813, was responsible for laying out two streets in the town – Swine or Millars Park, now known as Bank Street (on account of a branch of the National Bank opening there in 1825) and Darlings Haugh, now known as Bridge Street (opposite page). His proposal was that they should be one-sided streets with gardens opposite. The idea was thought to have been borrowed from the New Town of Edinburgh which was under construction at the time …

... This feature alas has now gone in Bridge Street with the erection of several buildings on the sites of the gardens. Bank Street, however, has been more fortunate, and although the site was used as allotments for many years it is now a well-kept garden, beautifully laid out with lawns, flower beds and seats for the public.

South Church Session in 1907 at the Grange, formerly the Church Manse, in the old town. It was here, during a period of convalescence, that the Rev. Nathaniel Patterson, Parish Minister from 1821 to 1833, wrote his well-known and informative book "The Manse Garden". "It is read" said Dr. James Hamilton of London, "for the sake of its poetry, wisdom and Christian kindness, where there are no gardens, and will be read for the sake of other days when there are no manses". It was said to be a classic of its kind and was well received by gardeners far beyond the town of its origin.

The Playhouse, Galashiels.

The Pavilion Cinema was the first built in Galashiels (1911) and was owned by Fyfe and Fyfe of Glasgow. Together with film shows the owners frequently brought the Rothesay Entertainers to Galashiels after the summer season was over. The pavilion was demolished in 1970 and the site used for the inevitable supermarket.

The Playhouse Cinema, seen here circa 1930, was opened in 1920. It was owned by the Galashiels Playhouse Company and was used for performances of the town's operatic society besides showing films. It was subsequently sold to ABC who unfortunately removed the stage and orchestra pit. Now owned by Kingsway Entertainments Ltd., it is still in use as a cinema.

Edinburgh Road at Buckholm, Galashiels

Until 1764 the only way to transport goods in and out of Galashiels was by panniers on horseback, but in that year a turnpike road to Edinburgh was opened on the west bank of the Gala Water. This allowed much more freedom of movement for local business as wagons were now taking the place of pack-horses, but even with the opening of a new shorter route on the other side of the river, the present Edinburgh Road, transport was still slow and laborious. The introduction of rail travel in 1849 resolved the problem for commerce, but unfortunately the Edinburgh Road, or A7 as it is now known, was not improved on for many years and is still a subject of controversy 24 years after the closure of the railway.

In the early days Buckholmside was described as a "weaving village" or a "suburb" of Galashiels separated by the river and about half a mile. The two communities were gradually joined over the years as new houses and mills were built during Galashiels' industrial development.

In 1791 Buckholmside was the site of a local brewery set up by, of all people, the Parish Minister, Dr. Douglas! It was not a success, however. In 1806 it was bought by Sanderson and Patterson, timber merchants, who started a business that was to last for over 150 years.

1878/79 was the first full season for the Gala club after the break-up with Melrose. In season 1877/78 the uniform of the club was recorded in the minute-book as being black and yellow striped jerseys, but by October 1877 the Melrose members of the club had broken away and formed their own club at the Greenyards, taking with them, it is believed, the minute-book, the club colours and the goal posts! Some justice was achieved though at the first meeting between the two teams after the split which took place in November 1878 and resulted in a win for Gala.

BORDER BOWLING TOURNAMENT. GALASHIELS. 1908.

Gala Bowling Club was opened on 2nd July 1859 at Kirkbrae. The first match was played against Selkirk on 13th August. Gala won by 4 shots. At the return match two weeks later Gala again won. The club moved to their present green at Scott Crescent in 1883 and Gala Waverly took over at Kirkbrae.

On this and the page opposite are two contrasting photographs of Market Street taken from virtually the same spot. The first sees the street as it was about 1899. The outstanding feature here is the old Victoria and Volunteer Arms Hotel dating from the middle of the 19th century. It was one of six hotels in the town which offered stabling facilities at that time.

MARKET ST. GALASHIELS.

This later photograph, taken in 1922, shows the street very much as it is today, 70 years on. The bridge was widened in 1910, about the same time that the Kings Temperance Hotel moved from the corner of Market Street and Bank Street to its present location.

This is the 4th K.O.S.B. football team before a game with Gala Fairydean. The only football to take place in the town during the 1914-18 war was between Gala Fairydean and armed forces teams, mainly the K.O.S.B. who were based in Gala and the Royal Scots based in Selkirk.

This 1906 postcard was sent out locally to advertise the availability of the band. Its pre-printed message reads: "On behalf of the Committee of the Galashiels EX-SOLDIERS ASSOCIATION I wish to draw your attention to our PIPE BAND. We are open to take on Engagements of any description, such as Picnics, Sunday School Treats, Choir Drives, Demonstrations, Flower Shows, Horse Shows, Garden Parties etc etc. The Band is composed of Six Pipers and Three Drummers and is equipped with a complete Highland Costume, supplied by Messrs. Hobson & Sons of London. We are prepared to submit to you terms for one or more Pipers if required, which can be had from any Member of Committee or the Secy. On behalf of the Ex-Soldiers Association. Yours respectfully, W. SANDERSON".

Galashiels · High Street

The Wrench Series No. 729

High Street in 1904.

26

Wilderhaugh at the turn of the century. The houses in the middle distance have now gone and the space is occupied by the large garage and showroom complex of Adam Purves and Sons. Very prominent in the photograph is Buckholmside Skinworks chimney. It was by far the tallest in the town and during the 1953 coronation it was decorated by a large sign reading "God Save the Queen" which was lit up at night.

Cycle parades were common throughout the Borders in the earlier part of this century. This remarkable 'vehicle' won 1st prize for Mr. T. Hislop in 1907.

A childrens' concert in "somebody's back green" in the Old Town. It would probably have been in aid of the Galashiels Comforts Fund, for servicemen of the town.

The Braw Lads Gathering. On the morning of 28th June 1930 it was estimated that about 10,000 people gathered at the Burgh Chambers to see the Burgh Crier Mr. G.K. Fox proclaim the Fair and the Provost handing over the Burgh Flag to the Braw Lad Mr. Henry Polson. The Braw Lad, with his Lass, Miss Hazel Gardiner, then led a cavalcade of 269 horses and riders which included the Coronets and Standard Bearers of other border towns. They proceeded to Netherdale Playing Fields where at 9.15 a.m. a ceremony took place commemorating the incident of 1337 at the Raid Stane. The riders thereafter crossed the Tweed and visited Abbotsford House at the invitation of General Maxwell-Scott.

READY FOR THE BRAW LADS' DAY IN SCOTT STREET

At 10.45 a.m. at the Mercat Cross the ceremony took place to commemorate the "Act of Sasine" of Ettrick Forest, of which Galashiels was then a part, to Margaret Tudor on the occasion of her marriage to King James IV of Scotland in 1503, an event which eventually led to the Union of the Crowns of Scotland and England in 1603. After visiting New Gala House at Mr. Scott's invitation the riders proceeded through the town to the Market Square. At 11.45 a.m. approx the Braw Lad performed the "Act of Homage" at the War Memorial in recognition of the sacrifice made by the people of Galashiels during the Great War.

The ceremonies have changed very little over the years although New Gala House is of course no longer visited and the number of attendants to the Braw Lad and Lass were reduced from eight to four some years ago.

Cottage Hospital, Galashiels.

A public meeting was held in 1891 and a committee appointed to put into effect the resolution to erect a cottage hospital on similar lines to those in other Borders towns. At length a site at Eastlands was agreed upon. It was designed by John Wallace, an Edinburgh architect and built by the local firm Robert Hall & Company. The hospital was formally opened in November 1893 free of debt thanks to the generosity of public subscribers.

In November 1891 an anonymous donor presented a house in Gala Terrace rent free to be used as a home for nurses so long as the institution in Galashiels remained a branch of the "Queen Victoria Jubilee Institute for Nurses".

The "Galashiels Cenotaph" was used for Remembrance Sunday Services until the opening of the War Memorial, which was unveiled by Field Marshall Earl Haig in October 1925. Designed by Sir Robert Lorimer (who also designed the fountain in Cornmill Square) the memorial takes the form of a Peel tower with a chiming clock, standing in front of which is the bronze figure of a Borderer on horseback. This is the work of Thomas Clapperton, a native of Galashiels and a sculptor of international repute.

A large bronze plaque contains the names of all 638 "Braw Lads" who fell during the First World War. Above this is the "Angel of Peace", so called on account of the effect of concealed lighting which seemed to give the figure angels' wings. Unfortunately modern lighting around Cornmill Square has meant that this effect is no longer possible. The angel was carved by Galashiels sculptor David Sutherland. In 1947, two further plaques, containing the names of those who were killed serving their country during the Second World War, were added.

Galashiels, Old Gala House, Edwards' Series

The house dates from around 1583 and was once home to the Lairds of Galashiels; the Pringles until 1632 and then the Scotts until 1876 when the family took up residence in New Gala House. During renovations in 1952, a magnificent painted ceiling, dated 1635, was discovered in one of the upper rooms. It is said to depict the marriage settlement between two local families. Gala house is still in use today, as a museum and art gallery, and is frequently used as a meeting place for local clubs and societies.

Galashiels   *Post Office and High Street*

In 1791 the Rev. Dr. Douglas remarked "that the need for a Post Office in Galashiels was much required". At this time all letters sent to Galashiels were addressed "near Melrose", "by Selkirk" or "by Stagehall". That same year a Post Office was established in Elm Row. The Postmaster was a merchant named James Brown and either he or a member of his family had to walk to Melrose in the morning and Clovenfords in the afternoon to collect the mail. For this he received three shillings and sixpence a week. The Post Office has since been located at Market Place, High Street and Bank Street. The present Post Office in Channel Street was opened by Provost Dickson in 1896.

The Tweed Mill was built in 1852 and traded under the name of P. and R. Sanderson. It was the first mill in Galashiels to be entirely powered by steam, as most of the water in the mill lade was being used by other factories. This photograph was taken around 1906. Over the years, the mill has housed various other businesses. Dobson's Dyeworks, later taken over by Kemp Blair and Co., were founded in 1920 and in 1938 Stewart Brothers Wool Brokers took over part of the mill as a store. The north end of the mill, known as the Pirns, was occupied by Andrew Stewart (Woollens) from 1945 until 1989 when it was converted into houses.

Peter Anderson bought the Huddersfield Mill in 1907 and changed the name to Bridge Mill. It remained with the Anderson family until 1962 when it was sold to John M. Buchan Ltd. In 1969, when Buchans moved to Abbotsford Mill, Bridge Mill was sold to the Post Office and subsequently demolished.

Roxburgh Street Public School, Galashiels
Valentine's Series

The Gala School, in Roxburgh Street, was run as a private enterprise from 1847 until 1873, when it was handed over to the School Board. This building (now named Roxburgh Street School) replaced the original building which was pulled down in 1892. In 1938, Roxburgh Street School united with the Academy in Melrose Road, to be known as the Junior Secondary and Senior Secondary respectively. In 1964, when both schools moved into the same building in Elm Row, this building was demolished.

"Oaklea House", in Melrose Road, became Galashiels New Academy in 1910 when the school was moved from its original site in Croft Street. At that time the school had about 150 pupils. The badge of the Academy, an eagle with the motto "I rise up with wings", is generally believed to have been inspired by two stone eagles which used to guard the front entrance. Work began to extend the building in 1940 and by 1942 the school had about 500 pupils. This building was in use until the school was transferred to Elm Row.

Although the weathervane on the Mercat Cross is dated 1695, the Cross has probably stood on or near this site from about the time that Galashiels became a Burgh of Barony. Nearly all of the buildings behind the cross have been demolished and replaced by modern housing developments. The first of these, completed in 1963, received a Saltire Society award for the best designed local authority houses in Scotland.

Eildon Hills from Melrose Road.

Melrose Road in 1906. The sprawling Langlee housing estate completely dominates this tranquil scene now. Work began in 1953 and over 1200 houses were built.

The children were never far away when the local photographer set up his camera. This picture dates from about 1906.

MEIGLE STREET, GALASHIELS

This view looks much the same today except for the rows of railings. These went during the Second World War in the drive for scrap iron. Meant as a morale booster for the home front, to make everyone feel involved in the war effort, the iron was never used. If only someone had bothered to label them all, they might have been returned to their owners after the war!

The fountain in Cornmill Square, in May 1913, only days before the official opening ceremony. A steam-roller is relaying the road surface in preparation for the big occasion. The New Square was built on the site of the old Cornmill, which was demolished in 1909. The fountain was designed by well known Edinburgh architect Sir Robert Lorimer.

Despite the apparent lack of activity, the building was indeed removed during one of the many road improvement schemes which were undertaken around this time.

This postcard was sent from Peebles in 1910 to the Eye Ward of Edinburgh Royal Infirmary. The message reads: "Your PC received what a pleasant surprise too. Glad it is over and hope successful. When are you going home. I go Monday and will expect to see you. love from Janet Having a fine holiday here."

Only the building on the right of this picture has escaped demolition, the site being prepared for industrial development. Although a factory unit was built on the right of the street, the area on the left is still an open space and is used as a car park.

Lawyer's Brae, Galashiels.

In 1873 a contract for a Public Library was placed with Messrs. Hall & Murray of Galashiels. The cost, including books, was met by public subscriptions. The Library was opened in October 1874 by local Member of Parliament G.O. Trevelyan. On the right of this 1905 photograph can be seen part of the old Cornmill.

At the top of this rooftop view of Ladhope Bank, is the old Glendinning Terrace School. It was erected in 1876 by the Melrose School Board (the part of Galashiels on the left bank of the river Gala was formerly in the parish of Melrose) and taken over by the Burgh School Board in 1891. The school was completely rebuilt in 1936.

7. NEAR ST. PETER'S CHURCH. GALASHIELS

Taken from Abbotsford Road, in 1914, this photograph looks towards the Old Town. The building on the left is the old St. Peter's Primary School which is now the Careers Service Regional Headquarters. Behind the group of people is the Gala Aisle with its original roof still intact.

This postcard shows the top of High Street after the record-breaking snow storm of December 1906. In rural areas some farms and villages were cut off for many days. The message reads: "I am sending you this P.C. to let you see what some of the streets looked like, but they were really worse than this!"

GALA PARK RD & ST ANDREW ST GALASHIELS

The houses on the left of the picture, known as "The Concretes" because of the building materials used, have been demolished and replaced by a modern block of flats. Otherwise, this scene has changed very little over the last 80 years.

A D.I.Y. superstore stands on the near side of the river today and it is hard to imagine that this industrial scene ever existed. The clock tower belonged to Sanderson & Murray Skinworks. At its peak, in the 1920s, the company employed 220 people but by the 1960s, due to the availability of new machinery, the workforce had fallen to 140. A fall in the demand for sheepskin products resulted in the closure of the factory in April 1980.

This view of Market Street, in 1905, is dominated by the Roman Catholic Church of Our Lady and St. Andrew. It was built in 1856 on the site of an earlier chapel and enlarged in 1873.

Left: A remarkable display outside fishmonger and poulterer J.P. Emslie's shop in Bank Street. What would the Environmental Health Inspectors have to say now about this little lot?

Right: The 148 word message crammed onto this postcard, which was sent to Canada in July 1925, reads: 'Dear Uncle, This is the hotel where we had lunch on the way to Melrose Abbey. All Scottish buildings are alike, dark grey stone and very perpendicular, and all very old, substantial and comfortable. I love Edinburgh – there are many monuments – 2 castles & it is very large. There are tramcars, horses and motor buses but few private cars and none as good as ours! The residences are charming – flowers in abundance & everything is so neat. The countryside is extremely beautiful – we motored over 100 miles in it yesterday – rolling hills & well cultivated. The Edinburgh students are very good to us and there are several dances and teas. Was at a reception for us in the City Chambers – the most formal function I ever was at, like Gov't House in Toronto. I am having a wonderful time – the trip is well worth the money. Write soon please, Mary'